family favorites
italian

Bath · New York · Singapore · Hong Kong · Cologne · Delhi · Melbourne

fresh tomato soup

ingredients

SERVES 4

1 tbsp. olive oil

1 lb 7 oz/650 g plum
    tomatoes

1 onion, cut into quarters

1 garlic clove, sliced thinly

1 celery stalk, chopped
    coarsely

18 fl oz/500 ml/generous
    2 cups chicken stock

2 oz/55 g dried anellini or
    other soup pasta

salt and pepper

fresh flat-leaf parsley,
    chopped, to garnish

method

1 Pour the olive oil into a large, heavy-bottom pan and add the tomatoes, onion, garlic, and celery. Cover and cook over low heat for 45 minutes, occasionally shaking the pan gently, until the mixture is pulpy.

2 Transfer the mixture to a food processor or blender and process to a smooth purée. Push the purée through a strainer into a clean pan.

3 Add the stock and bring to a boil. Add the pasta, bring back to a boil, and cook for 8–10 minutes, until the pasta is tender but still firm to the bite. Season to taste with salt and pepper. Ladle into warmed bowls, sprinkle with the parsley, and serve immediately.

minestrone

ingredients

SERVES 4

3 tbsp. olive oil

2 onions, chopped

1/2 small green or savoy
cabbage, thick stems
removed and leaves
shredded

2 zucchini, chopped

2 celery stalks, chopped

2 carrots, chopped

2 potatoes, chopped

4 large tomatoes, peeled
and chopped

4 oz/115 g dried Great
Northern beans, soaked
overnight in enough cold
water to cover

2 pints/1.2 litres/5 cups
chicken or
vegetable stock

4 oz/115 g dried soup pasta

salt and pepper

freshly shaved Parmesan
cheese, to garnish

4 tbsp. freshly grated
Parmesan cheese,
to serve

method

1 Heat the oil in a large heavy-bottomed pan. Add the onions and cook over low heat, stirring occasionally, for 5 minutes, or until softened.

2 Add the cabbage, zucchini, celery, carrots, potatoes, and tomatoes to the pan, cover, and cook, stirring occasionally, for 10 minutes.

3 Drain and rinse the beans, then add to the pan. Pour in the stock, bring to a boil, cover, and simmer for 1–1 1/2 hours, or until the beans are tender.

4 Add the soup pasta to the pan and cook, uncovered, for 8–10 minutes, or until tender but still firm to the bite. Season to taste with salt and pepper and ladle into warmed bowls. Garnish with fresh Parmesan cheese shavings and an extra sprinkling of pepper. Serve, handing around the grated Parmesan cheese separately.

warm vegetable medley

ingredients

SERVES 4

4 tbsp. olive oil

2 celery stalks, sliced

2 red onions, sliced

450 g/1 lb eggplant, diced

1 garlic clove, chopped finely

5 plum tomatoes, chopped

3 tbsp. red wine vinegar

1 tbsp. sugar

3 tbsp. green olives, pitted

2 tbsp. capers

salt and pepper

4 tbsp. chopped fresh flat-leaf
    parsley

ciabatta or panini, to serve

method

1 Heat half the olive oil in a large, heavy-bottom pan. Add the celery and onions and cook over low heat, stirring occasionally, for 5 minutes, until softened but not colored. Add the remaining oil and the eggplant. Cook, stirring frequently, for about 5 minutes, until the eggplant starts to color.

2 Add the garlic, tomatoes, vinegar, and sugar, and mix well. Cover the mixture with a circle of waxed paper and let simmer gently for about 10 minutes.

3 Remove the waxed paper, stir in the olives and capers, and season to taste with salt and pepper. Pour into a serving dish and set aside to cool to room temperature. Sprinkle the parsley over the vegetables and serve with fresh bread or rolls.

warm pasta salad

ingredients

SERVES 4

8 oz/225 g dried farfalle or
    other pasta shapes
6 pieces of sun-dried tomato
    in oil, drained and chopped
4 scallions, chopped
2 oz/55 g arugula, shredded
1/2 cucumber, seeded and diced
2 tbsp. freshly grated
    Parmesan cheese
salt and pepper

dressing

4 tbsp. olive oil
1/2 tsp. superfine sugar
1 tbsp. white wine vinegar
1 tsp. Dijon mustard
4 fresh basil leaves,
    finely shredded
salt and pepper

method

1 To make the dressing, whisk the olive oil, sugar, vinegar, and mustard together in a bowl. Season to taste with salt and pepper. Stir in the basil.

2 Bring a large, heavy-bottom pan of lightly salted water to a boil. Add the pasta, return to a boil, and cook for 8–10 minutes, or until tender but still firm to the bite. Drain and transfer to a salad bowl. Add the dressing and toss well.

3 Add the chopped sun-dried tomatoes, scallions, arugula, and cucumber, season to taste with salt and pepper, and toss. Sprinkle with the Parmesan cheese and serve warm

three-color salad

ingredients

SERVES 4

10 oz/280 g mozzarella di
   bufala, drained and
   sliced thinly
8 plum tomatoes, sliced
salt and pepper
20 fresh basil leaves
4 fl oz/125 ml/1/2 cup extra-
   virgin olive oil

method

1 Arrange the cheese and tomato slices on 4 individual serving plates and season to taste with salt. Set aside in a cool place for 30 minutes.

2 Sprinkle the basil leaves over the salad and drizzle with the olive oil. Season with pepper and serve immediately.

spaghetti with meatballs

ingredients

SERVES 6

1 potato, diced

14 oz/400 g/1¾ cups
    ground steak

1 onion, finely chopped

1 egg

4 tbsp. chopped fresh flat-leaf
    parsley

all-purpose flour, for dusting

5 tbsp. virgin olive oil

14 fl oz/400 ml/1¾ cups
    strained tomatoes

2 tbsp. tomato paste

14 oz/400 g dried spaghetti

salt and pepper

for the garnish

6 fresh basil leaves, shredded

freshly grated Parmesan cheese

method

1 Place the potato in a small pan, add cold water to cover and a pinch of salt, and bring to a boil. Cook for 10–15 minutes, until tender, then drain. Either mash thoroughly with a potato masher or fork or pass through a potato ricer.

2 Combine the potato, steak, onion, egg, and parsley in a bowl and season to taste with salt and pepper. Spread out the flour on a plate. With dampened hands, shape the meat mixture into walnut-size balls and roll in the flour. Shake off any excess.

3 Heat the oil in a heavy-bottom skillet, add the meatballs, and cook over medium heat, stirring and turning frequently, for 8–10 minutes, until golden all over.

4 Add the strained tomatoes and tomato paste and cook for an additional 10 minutes, until the sauce is reduced and thickened.

5 Meanwhile, bring a large pan of lightly salted water to a boil. Add the pasta, bring back to a boil, and cook for 8–10 minutes, until tender but still firm to the bite.

6 Drain well and add to the meatball sauce, tossing well to coat. Transfer to a warmed serving dish, garnish with the basil leaves and Parmesan, and serve immediately.

spaghetti bolognese

ingredients

SERVES 4

2 tbsp. olive oil

1 tbsp. butter

1 small onion, finely chopped

1 carrot, finely chopped

1 celery stalk, finely chopped

1³/4 oz/50 g mushrooms, diced

8 oz/225 g ground beef

2³/4 oz/75 g unsmoked bacon
    or ham, diced

2 chicken livers, chopped

2 tbsp. tomato paste

14 fl oz/125 ml/¹/2 cup dry
    white wine

¹/2 tsp. freshly grated nutmeg

10 fl oz/300 ml/1¹/4 cups
    chicken stock

4 fl oz/125 ml/¹/2 cup heavy
    cream

1 lb/450 g dried spaghetti

salt and pepper

2 tbsp. chopped fresh
    flat-leaf parsley, to garnish

freshly grated Parmesan,
    to serve

method

1 Heat the olive oil and butter in a large pan over medium heat. Add the onion, carrot, celery, and mushrooms to the pan, then cook until soft. Add the beef and bacon and cook until the beef is evenly browned.

2 Stir in the chicken livers and tomato paste and cook for 2–3 minutes. Pour in the wine and season with salt, pepper, and the nutmeg. Add the stock. Bring to a boil, then cover and simmer gently over low heat for 1 hour. Stir in the cream and simmer, uncovered, until reduced.

3 Bring a large pan of lightly salted water to a boil. Add the pasta, return to a boil, and cook until tender but still firm to the bite. Drain and transfer to a warmed serving dish.

4 Spoon the meat sauce over the pasta, garnish with parsley, and serve with Parmesan cheese.

grilled steak with tomatoes & garlic

ingredients

SERVES 4

3 tbsp. olive oil, plus extra
for brushing

1 lb 9 oz/700 g tomatoes,
peeled and chopped

1 red bell pepper, seeded
and chopped

1 onion, chopped

2 garlic cloves, chopped finely

1 tbsp. chopped fresh flat-leaf
parsley

1 tsp. dried oregano

1 tsp. sugar

salt and pepper

4 6-oz/175-g entrecôte or
rump steaks

method

1 Place the oil, tomatoes, red bell pepper, onion, garlic, parsley, oregano, and sugar in a heavy-bottom pan and season to taste with salt and pepper. Bring to a boil, reduce the heat, and let simmer for 15 minutes.

2 Meanwhile, trim any fat around the outsides of the steaks. Season each generously with pepper (but no salt) and brush with olive oil. Cook on a preheated grill pan according to taste: 2–3 minutes each side for rare; 3–4 minutes each side for medium 4–5 minutes on each side for well done.

3 Transfer the steaks to warmed individual plates and spoon the sauce over them. Serve immediately.

baked lasagna

ingredients

SERVES 4

for the meat sauce

3 tbsp. olive oil

1 onion, chopped finely

1 celery stick, chopped finely

1 carrot, chopped finely

3 1/2 oz/100 g pancetta,
    chopped finely

6 oz/175 g/3/4 cup
    ground beef

6 oz/175 g/3/4 cup
    ground pork

3 1/2 fl oz/100 ml/scant
    1/2 cup dry red wine

1/4 pint/150 ml/2/3 cup
    beef stock

1 tbsp. tomato paste

salt and pepper

1 clove

1 bay leaf

1/4 pint/150 ml/2/3 cup
    boiling milk

14 oz/400 g dried
    lasagna verdi

1 quantity béchamel sauce
    (see page 44)

5 oz/140 g mozzarella cheese

5 oz/140 g freshly grated
    Parmesan cheese

2 oz/55 g unsalted butter,
    diced

method

1 First, make the meat sauce. Heat the olive oil in a large, heavy-bottom pan. Add the onion, celery, carrot, pancetta, beef, and pork, and cook over medium heat, stirring frequently and breaking up the meat with a wooden spoon, for 10 minutes, until lightly browned.

2 Add the wine, bring to a boil, and cook until reduced. Add about two-thirds of the stock, bring to a boil, and cook until reduced. Combine the remaining stock and tomato paste and add to the pan. Season to taste, add the clove, the bay leaf, and pour in the milk. Cover and let simmer over low heat for 1 1/2 hours.

3 Unless you are using lasagna that needs no precooking, bring a large pan of lightly salted water to a boil. Add the lasagna sheets, in batches, bring back to a boil, and cook for about 10 minutes, until tender but still firm to the bite. Remove with tongs and spread out on a clean dish towel.

4 Remove the meat sauce from the heat and discard the clove and bay leaf. Lightly grease a large, oven-proof dish with butter. Place a layer of the pasta in the base and cover it with a layer of meat sauce. Spoon a layer of béchamel sauce on top and sprinkle with one-third of the mozzarella and Parmesan cheeses. Continue making layers until all the ingredients are used, ending with a topping of béchamel sauce and sprinkled cheese Dot the top of the lasagna with the diced butter and bake in a preheated oven, 400°F/200°C, for 30 minutes, until golden and bubbling.

meatball surprise

ingredients

SERVES 8

1 lb 2 oz/500 g ground steak

1 lb 2 oz/500 g ground pork

2 garlic cloves, chopped
   finely

2 oz/55 g/1 cup fresh bread
   crumbs

1 3/4 oz/50 g/scant 1/2 cup
   freshly grated Parmesan
   cheese

1 tsp. dried oregano

1/2 tsp. ground cinnamon

grated rind and juice of
   1 lemon

2 eggs, beaten lightly

5 1/2 oz/150 g fontina cheese

6 tbsp. virgin olive oil

5 oz/140 g/1 1/4 cups dried,
   uncolored bread crumbs

salt and pepper

fresh flat-leaf parsley sprigs,
   to garnish

tomato sauce (see page 28),
   to serve

method

1 Combine the steak, pork, garlic, fresh bread crumbs, Parmesan, oregano, cinnamon, and lemon rind in a bowl. Stir in the lemon juice and beaten eggs, season with salt and pepper, and mix well.

2 Knead the mixture with dampened hands, then shape small quantities into 16 balls.

3 Cut the fontina into 16 cubes and press 1 cube into each meatball, then reshape them to enclose the cheese completely.

4 Heat the olive oil in a large, heavy-bottom skillet. Meanwhile, spread out the dried bread crumbs on a shallow plate and roll the meatballs in them to coat.

5 Add the meatballs, in batches, to the skillet and cook until golden brown all over. Transfer to an ovenproof dish using a slotted spoon and bake in a preheated oven, 350°F/180°C, for 15–20 minutes, until cooked through. Serve immediately, garnished with parsley sprigs and accompanied with tomato sauce.

cannelloni with spinach & ricotta

ingredients

SERVES 4

12 dried cannelloni tubes,
  3-in long
butter, for greasing

for the filling

5 oz/140 g lean ham,
  chopped
5 oz/140 g/3/4 cup frozen
  spinach, thawed and
  drained
4 oz/115 g/scant 1/2 cup
  ricotta cheese
1 egg
3 tbsp. freshly grated pecorino
  cheese
pinch of freshly grated nutmeg
salt and pepper

for the cheese sauce

1 pint/600 ml/21/2 cups milk
1 oz/25 g unsalted butter
2 tbsp. all-purpose flour
3 oz/85 g/3/4 cup freshly
  grated Gruyère cheese
salt and pepper

method

1 Bring a large pan of lightly salted water to a boil. Add the cannelloni tubes, bring back to a boil, and cook for 6–7 minutes, until nearly tender. Drain and rinse under cold water. Spread out the tubes on a clean dish towel.

2 Put the ham, spinach, and ricotta into a food processor and process for a few seconds until combined. Add the egg and pecorino and process again to a smooth paste. Scrape the filling into a bowl and season to taste with nutmeg, salt, and pepper. Grease an ovenproof dish with butter. Spoon the filling into a pastry bag fitted with a 1/2-inch nozzle. Carefully open one cannelloni tube, stand it upright, and pipe in the filling. Place the filled tube in the dish and continue to fill the remaining cannelloni.

3 For the cheese sauce, heat the milk to just below boiling point. Meanwhile, melt the butter in another pan. Add the flour to the butter and cook over low heat, stirring constantly, for 1 minute. Remove the pan from the heat and gradually stir in the hot milk. Return the pan to the heat and bring to a boil, stirring constantly. Let simmer over the lowest possible heat, stirring frequently, for 10 minutes, until thickened. Remove the pan from the heat, stir in the Gruyère, and season. Spoon the cheese sauce over the filled cannelloni. Cover the dish with foil and bake in a preheated oven, 350°F/180°C, for 20–25 minutes. Serve immediately.

spaghetti alla carbonara

ingredients

SERVES 4

1 lb/450 g dried spaghetti

1 tbsp. olive oil

8 oz/225 g rindless pancetta
or lean bacon, chopped

4 eggs

5 tbsp. light cream

4 tbsp. freshly grated
Parmesan cheese

salt and pepper

method

1 Bring a large, heavy-bottom pan of lightly salted water to a boil. Add the pasta, return to a boil, and cook for 8–10 minutes, or until tender but still firm to the bite.

2 Meanwhile, heat the olive oil in a heavy-bottom skillet. Add the chopped pancetta and cook over medium heat, stirring frequently, for 8–10 minutes.

3 Beat the eggs with the cream in a small bowl and season to taste with salt and pepper. Drain the pasta and return it to the pan. Tip in the contents of the skillet, then add the egg mixture and half the Parmesan cheese. Stir well, then transfer to a warmed serving dish. Serve immediately, sprinkled with the remaining Parmesan cheese.

pepperoni pasta

ingredients

SERVES 4

3 tbsp. olive oil

1 onion, chopped

1 red bell pepper, seeded and
    diced

1 orange bell pepper, seeded
    and diced

1 lb 12 oz/800 g canned
    chopped tomatoes

1 tbsp. sun-dried tomato paste

1 tsp. paprika

8 oz/225 g pepperoni, sliced

2 tbsp. chopped fresh
    flat-leaf parsley, plus extra
    to garnish

1 lb/450 g dried garganelli

salt and pepper

mixed salad greens,
    to serve

method

1 Heat 2 tablespoons of the olive oil in a large, heavy-bottom skillet. Add the onion and cook over low heat, stirring occasionally, for 5 minutes, or until softened. Add the red and orange bell peppers, tomatoes and their can juices, sun-dried tomato paste, and paprika to the pan and bring to a boil.

2 Add the pepperoni and parsley and season to taste with salt and pepper. Stir well and bring to a boil, then reduce the heat and simmer for 10–15 minutes.

3 Meanwhile, bring a large, heavy-bottom pan of lightly salted water to a boil. Add the pasta, return to a boil, and cook for 8–10 minutes, or until tender but still firm to the bite. Drain well and transfer to a warmed serving dish. Add the remaining olive oil and toss. Add the sauce and toss again. Sprinkle with parsley and serve immediately with mixed salad greens.

four seasons pizza

ingredients

SERVES 2

pizza dough (see page 40)

plain flour, for dusting

for the tomato sauce

2 tbsp. olive oil

1 small onion, chopped finely

1 garlic clove, chopped finely

1 red bell pepper, seeded and
   chopped

8 oz/225 g plum tomatoes,
   peeled and chopped

1 tbsp. tomato paste

1 tsp. soft brown sugar

1 tbsp. shredded fresh basil

1 bay leaf

salt and pepper

for the topping

2½ oz cooked shrimp

2 oz bottled artichoke hearts,
   sliced thinly

1 oz mozzarella cheese,
   drained and sliced thinly

1 tomato, sliced thinly

3½ oz/100 g mushrooms or
   pepperoni, sliced thinly

2 tsp. capers, rinsed

2 tsp. pitted, sliced black olives

2 tbsp. olive oil

salt and pepper

method

1 To make the tomato sauce, heat the olive oil in a heavy-bottom pan. Add the onion, garlic, and bell pepper, and cook over low heat, stirring occasionally, for 5 minutes, until softened. Add the tomatoes, tomato paste, sugar, basil, and bay leaf, and season to taste with salt and pepper. Cover and let simmer, stirring occasionally, for 30 minutes, until thickened. Remove the pan from the heat and let the sauce cool completely.

2 Turn out the prepared pizza dough onto a lightly floured counter and knock down. Knead briefly, then cut it in half and roll out each piece into a circle about ¼ inch/0.75 cm thick. Transfer to a lightly oiled baking sheet and push up the edges with your fingers to form a small rim.

3 Spread the tomato sauce over the pizza bases, almost to the edge. Cover one-quarter with shrimp. Cover a second quarter with sliced artichoke hearts. Cover the third quarter with alternate slices of mozzarella and tomato. Cover the final quarter with sliced mushrooms or pepperoni. Sprinkle the surface with capers and olives, season to taste with salt and pepper, and drizzle with the olive oil.

4 Bake in a preheated oven, 425°F/220°C, for 20–25 minutes, until the crust is crisp and the cheese has melted. Serve immediately.

roast lamb with rosemary & marsala

ingredients

SERVES 6

4 lb/1.8 kg leg of lamb

2 garlic cloves, sliced thinly

2 tbsp. rosemary leaves

8 tbsp. olive oil

salt and pepper

2 lb/900 g potatoes, cut into
    1-inch/2.5-cm cubes

6 fresh sage leaves, chopped

1/4 pint/150 ml/2/3 cup
    Marsala

method

1 Use a small, sharp knife to make incisions all over the lamb, opening them out slightly to make little pockets. Insert the garlic slices and about half the rosemary leaves in the pockets.

2 Place the lamb in a roasting pan and spoon half the olive oil over it. Roast in a preheated oven, 425°F/220°C, for 15 minutes. Reduce the oven temperature to 350°F/180°C. Remove the lamb from the oven and season to taste with salt and pepper. Turn the lamb over, return to the oven, and roast for an additional hour.

3 Meanwhile, spread out the cubed potatoes in a second roasting pan, pour the remaining olive oil over them, and toss to coat. Sprinkle with the remaining rosemary and the sage. Place the potatoes in the oven with the lamb and roast for 40 minutes.

4 Remove the lamb from the oven, turn it over, and pour over the Marsala. Return it to the oven with the potatoes and cook for an additional 15 minutes.

5 Transfer the lamb to a carving board and cover with foil. Place the roasting pan over high heat and bring the juices to a boil. Continue to boil until thickened and syrupy. Strain into a warmed gravy boat or pitcher. Carve the lamb into slices and serve with the potatoes and sauce.

lamb shanks with roasted onions

ingredients

SERVES 4

4 12-oz/350 g lamb shanks

6 garlic cloves

2 tbsp. virgin olive oil

1 tbsp. very finely chopped
    fresh rosemary

salt and pepper

4 red onions

12 oz/350 g carrots, cut into
    thin sticks

4 tbsp. water

method

1 Trim off any excess fat from the lamb. Using a small, sharp knife, make 6 incisions in each shank. Cut the garlic cloves lengthwise into 4 slices. Insert 6 garlic slices in the incisions in each lamb shank.

2 Place the lamb in a single layer in a roasting pan, drizzle with the olive oil, sprinkle with the rosemary, and season with pepper. Roast in a preheated oven, 350°F/180°C, for 45 minutes.

3 Wrap each onion in a square of foil. Remove the lamb shanks from the oven and season with salt. Return the pan to the oven and place the onions on the shelf next to it. Roast for an additional 1 hour, or until the lamb is tender.

4 Meanwhile, bring a large pan of water to a boil. Add the carrot sticks and blanch for 1 minute. Drain and refresh under cold water.

5 Remove the roasting pan from the oven when the lamb is meltingly tender and transfer it to a warmed serving dish. Skim off any fat from the roasting pan and place it over medium heat. Add the carrots and cook for 2 minutes, then add the water, bring to a boil, and let simmer, stirring constantly and scraping up the glazed bits from the bottom of the roasting pan.

6 Transfer the carrots and sauce to the serving dish. Remove the onions from the oven and unwrap. Cut off and discard about 1/2 inch/1.25 cm of the tops and add the onions to the dish. Serve immediately.

spaghetti with roasted garlic & pepper sauce

ingredients

SERVES 4

6 large garlic cloves,
   unpeeled
14 oz/400 g bottled roasted
   red bell peppers, drained
   and sliced
7 oz/200 g canned chopped
   tomatoes
3 tbsp. olive oil
1/4 tsp. dried chili flakes
1 tsp. chopped fresh thyme
   or oregano
salt and pepper
12 oz/350 g dried spaghetti,
   bucatini, or linguine
freshly grated Parmesan,
   to serve

method

1 Place the unpeeled garlic cloves in a shallow, ovenproof dish. Roast in a preheated oven at 400°F/200°C for 7–10 minutes, or until the cloves feel soft.

2 Put the bell peppers, tomatoes, and oil in a food processor or blender, then purée. Squeeze the garlic flesh into the purée. Add the chili flakes and oregano. Season with salt and pepper. Blend again, then scrape into a pan and set aside.

3 Cook the pasta in plenty of boiling salted water until al dente. Drain and transfer to a warm serving dish. Reheat the sauce and pour over the pasta. Toss well to mix. Serve at once with parmesan.

creamy chicken ravioli

ingredients

SERVES 4

4 oz/115 g cooked skinless,
   boneless chicken breast,
   coarsely chopped
2 oz/55 g cooked spinach
2 oz/55 g prosciutto, coarsely
   chopped
1 shallot, coarsely chopped
6 tbsp. freshly grated romano
   cheese
pinch of freshly grated nutmeg
2 eggs, lightly beaten
1 quantity basic pasta dough
   (see page 46, omitting
   spinach from the recipe)
all-purpose flour, for dusting
10 fl oz/300 ml/1¼ cups
   heavy cream or panna
   da cucina
2 garlic cloves, finely chopped
4 oz/115 g cremini mushrooms,
   thinly sliced
2 tbsp. shredded fresh basil
salt and pepper
fresh basil sprigs, to garnish

method

1 Place the chicken, spinach, prosciutto, and shallot in a food processor and process until chopped and blended. Transfer to a bowl, stir in 2 tablespoons of the romano cheese, the nutmeg, and half the egg. Season to taste with salt and pepper.

2 Halve the pasta dough. Wrap one piece in plastic wrap and thinly roll out the other on a lightly floured counter. Cover with a dish towel and roll out the second piece of dough. Place small mounds of the filling in rows 1½ inches/4 cm apart on one sheet of dough and brush the spaces in between with beaten egg. Lift the second piece of dough to fit on top. Press down firmly between the mounds of filling, pushing out any air. Cut into squares and place on a floured dish towel. Let the ravioli rest for 1 hour.

3 Bring a large pan of lightly salted water to a boil. Add the ravioli, in batches, return to a boil, and cook for 5 minutes. Remove with a slotted spoon and drain on paper towels, then transfer to a warmed dish.

4 Meanwhile, to make the sauce, pour the cream into a skillet, add the garlic, and bring to a boil. Simmer for 1 minute, then add the mushrooms and 2 tablespoons of the remaining cheese. Season to taste and simmer for 3 minutes. Stir in the basil, then pour the sauce over the ravioli. Sprinkle with the remaining cheese, garnish with basil sprigs, and serve.

chicken tortellini

ingredients

SERVES 4

4 oz/115 g boned chicken
   breast, skinned

2 oz/55 g prosciutto

1 1/2 oz/40 g cooked spinach,
   well drained

1 tbsp. finely chopped onion

2 tbsp. freshly grated
   Parmesan cheese

pinch of ground allspice

1 egg, beaten

1 lb/450 g basic pasta dough
   (see page 46, omitting
   spinach from the recipe)

salt and pepper

2 tbsp. chopped fresh
   parsley, to garnish

sauce

10 fl oz/300 ml/1 1/4 cups
   light cream

2 garlic cloves, crushed

4 oz/115 g white mushrooms,
   thinly sliced

4 tbsp. freshly grated
   Parmesan cheese

method

1 Bring a pan of salted water to a boil. Add the chicken and poach for about 10 minutes. Let cool slightly, then place in a food processor with the prosciutto, spinach, and onion and process until finely chopped. Stir in the Parmesan cheese, allspice, and egg and season with salt and pepper to taste.

2 Thinly roll out the pasta dough and cut into 1 1/2–2-inch/4–5-cm circles.

3 Place 1/2 teaspoon of the chicken and ham filling in the center of each circle. Fold the pieces in half and press the edges to seal, then wrap each piece round your index finger, cross over the ends, and curl the rest of the dough backward to make a navel shape. Re-roll the trimmings and repeat until all of the dough is used up.

4 Bring a pan of salted water to a boil. Add the tortellini, in batches, return to a boil and cook for 5 minutes. Drain the tortellini well and transfer to a serving dish.

5 To make the sauce, bring the cream and garlic to a boil in a small pan, then simmer for 3 minutes. Add the mushrooms and half of the cheese, season to taste with salt and pepper, and simmer for 2–3 minutes. Pour the sauce over the tortellini. Sprinkle over the remaining Parmesan cheese, garnish with the parsley, and serve.

cheese & tomato pizza

ingredients

SERVES 2

for the dough

8 oz/225 g/1½ cups all-
purpose flour, plus extra
for dusting

1 tsp. salt

1 tsp. active dry yeast

1 tbsp. olive oil, plus extra for
brushing

6 tbsp. lukewarm water

for the topping

6 tomatoes, sliced thinly

6 oz/175 g/mozzarella
cheese, drained and
sliced thinly

salt and pepper

2 tbsp. shredded fresh basil
leaves

2 tbsp. olive oil

method

1 To make the pizza dough, sift the flour and salt into a bowl and stir in the yeast. Make a well in the center and pour in the oil and water. Gradually incorporate the dry ingredients into the liquid, using a wooden spoon or floured hands.

2 Turn out the dough onto a lightly floured counter and knead well for 5 minutes, until smooth and elastic. Return to the clean bowl, covered with lightly oiled plastic wrap, and set aside to rise in a warm place for about 1 hour, or until doubled in size.

3 Turn out the dough onto a lightly floured counter and knock down. Knead briefly, then cut it in half and roll out each piece into a circle about ¼ inch/0.75 cm thick. Transfer to a lightly oiled baking sheet and push up the edges with your fingers to form a small rim.

4 For the topping, arrange the tomato and mozzarella slices alternately over the pizza bases. Season to taste with salt and pepper, sprinkle with the basil, and drizzle with the olive oil.

5 Bake in a preheated oven, 450°F/230°C, for 15–20 minutes, until the crust is crisp and the cheese has melted. Serve immediately.

spaghetti with clams

ingredients

SERVES 4

2 lb 4 oz/1 kg live clams

6 fl oz/175 ml/3/4 cup water

6 fl oz/175 ml/3/4 cup dry
   white wine

12 oz/350 g dried spaghetti

5 tbsp. olive oil

2 garlic cloves, chopped finely

4 tbsp. chopped fresh flat-leaf
   parsley

salt and pepper

method

1 Scrub the clams under cold running water and discard any with broken or damaged shells or those that do not shut when sharply tapped. Place the clams in a large, heavy-bottom pan, add the water and wine, cover, and cook over high heat, shaking the pan occasionally, for 5 minutes, until the shells have opened.

2 Remove the clams with a slotted spoon and set aside to cool slightly. Strain the cooking liquid through a cheesecloth-lined strainer into a small pan. Bring to a boil and cook until reduced by about half and remove from heat. Meanwhile, discard any clams that have not opened, remove the remainder from their shells, and set aside.

3 Bring a large pan of lightly salted water to a boil. Add the pasta, bring back to a boil, and cook for 8–10 minutes, until tender but still firm to the bite.

4 Meanwhile, heat the olive oil in a large, heavy-bottom skillet. Add the garlic and cook, stirring frequently, for 2 minutes. Add the parsley and the reduced cooking liquid and let simmer gently.

5 Drain the pasta and add it to the skillet with the clams. Season to taste with salt and pepper and cook, stirring constantly, for 4 minutes, until the pasta is coated and the clams have heated through. Transfer to a warmed serving dish and serve immediately.

baked pasta with mushrooms

ingredients

SERVES 4

3 oz/85 g butter, plus extra for
    greasing
12 oz/350 g mixed exotic
    mushrooms, sliced
12 oz/350 g dried tagliatelle
2 egg yolks
salt and pepper
4 tbsp. freshly grated
    pecorino cheese

for the béchamel sauce

2 oz/55 g unsalted butter
2 oz/55 g/3/8 cup all-purpose
    flour
18 fl oz/500 ml/generous
    2 cups milk
1 bay leaf
salt and pepper
pinch of freshly grated nutmeg
5 oz/140 g fontina cheese,
    sliced thinly

method

1 To make the béchamel sauce, melt the butter, add the flour, and cook over low heat, stirring constantly, for 1 minute. Remove the pan from the heat and gradually stir in the milk. Return the pan to the heat and bring to a boil, stirring constantly, until thickened and smooth.

2 Add the bay leaf and let simmer gently for 2 minutes. Remove the bay leaf and season the sauce to taste with salt, pepper, and nutmeg. Remove the pan from the heat. Stir in the fontina cheese and set aside.

3 Melt 1 oz/28 g of the butter in a large pan. Add the mushrooms and cook over low heat, stirring occasionally, for 10 minutes.

4 Meanwhile, bring a large pan of lightly salted water to a boil. Add the pasta, bring back to a boil, and cook for 8–10 minutes, until tender but still firm to the bite. Drain, return to the pan, and add the remaining butter, the egg yolks, and about one-third of the béchamel sauce, then season to taste with salt and pepper. Toss well to mix, then gently stir in the mushrooms.

5 Lightly grease a large, ovenproof dish and spoon in the pasta mixture. Pour over the remaining sauce evenly and sprinkle with the grated pecorino. Bake in a preheated oven, 400°F/200°C, for 15–20 minutes, until golden brown. Serve immediately.

spinach & ricotta ravioli

ingredients

SERVES 4

12 oz/350 g fresh spinach
    leaves, coarse stalks
    removed
8 oz/225 g/1 cup ricotta
    cheese
2 oz/55 g/1/2 cup freshly
    grated Parmesan cheese
2 eggs, lightly beaten
pinch of freshly grated nutmeg
pepper
all-purpose flour, for dusting
freshly grated Parmesan
    cheese, to serve (optional)

spinach pasta dough

1 1/3 cups white all-purpose
    flour, plus extra for dusting
pinch of salt
8 oz/225 g frozen spinach,
    thawed, squeezed dry,
    and finely chopped
2 eggs, lightly beaten
1 tbsp olive oil

method

1 To make the pasta dough, sift the flour into a food processor and add the salt. Add the chopped spinach, then pour in the eggs and olive oil and process until the dough begins to come together. Turn out onto a lightly floured counter and knead until smooth. Wrap in plastic wrap and let rest for at least 30 minutes.

2 Cook the spinach, with just the water clinging to the leaves after washing, over low heat for 5 minutes until wilted. Drain and squeeze out as much moisture as possible. Cool, then chop finely. Beat the ricotta cheese until smooth, then stir in the spinach, Parmesan, and half the egg and season to taste with nutmeg and pepper.

3 Halve the pasta dough. Cover one piece and thinly roll out the other on a floured counter. Cover and roll out the second piece. Put small mounds of filling in rows 1 1/2 inches/4 cm apart on one sheet of dough and brush the spaces in between with the remaining beaten egg. Lift the second piece of dough to fit on top. Press down between the mounds, pushing out any air. Cut into squares and rest on a dish towel for 1 hour.

4 Bring a large pan of salted water to a boil, add the ravioli, in batches, return to a boil, and cook for 5 minutes. Remove with a slotted spoon and drain on paper towels. Serve with grated Parmesan cheese, if liked.

This edition published by Parragon in 2008

Parragon
Queen Street House
4 Queen Street
Bath BA1 1HE, UK

Copyright © Parragon Books Ltd 2008

ISBN 978-1-4075-1880-0

Printed in China

Notes for the reader
• This book uses both imperial, metric, and US cup measurements. Follow the same units of measurement throughout; do not mix imperial and metric.
• All spoon measurements are level; teaspoons are assumed to be 5 ml and tablespoons are assumed to be 15 ml.
• Unless otherwise stated, milk is assumed to be full fat, eggs and other individual fruits such as bananas are medium, and pepper is freshly ground black pepper.
• Some recipes contain nuts. If you are allergic to nuts you should avoid them and any products containing nuts. Recipes using raw or very lightly cooked eggs should be avoided by infants, the elderly, pregnant women, convalescents and anyone suffering from an illness.